Want free goodies?
Email us at freebies@honeybadgercoloring.com

 @HoneyBadgerColoring

 @Honey Badger Coloring

Shop our other books at
www.honeybadgercoloring.com
Wholesale distribution through Ingram Content Group
www.ingramcontent.com/publishers/distribution/wholesale
For questions and customer service, email us at
support@honeybadgercoloring.com

Initial Planning Phase

IDEAS FOR THEME

IDEAS FOR VENUE

IDEAS FOR COLORS

IDEAS FOR MUSIC

IDEAS FOR RECEPTION

OTHER IDEAS

Notes & Ideas

Wedding Budget Planner

Expense MANAGER

CATEGORY/ITEMS	BUDGET	ACTUAL COST	BALANCE

Wedding Budget Checklist

CATEGORY	BUDGET	ACTUAL COST	DEPOSIT	BALANCE

Wedding Contact List

IMPORTANT VENDOR CONTACTS

	NAME	PHONE #	EMAIL	ADDRESS
OFFICIANT				
RECEPTION VENUE				
BRIDAL SHOP				
SEAMSTRESS				
FLORIST				
CATERER				
DJ/ENTERTAINMENT				
WEDDING VENUE				
TRANSPORTATION				
OTHER:				
OTHER:				
OTHER:				

NOTES & More

SPECIAL REMINDERS

Planning Snapshot

CEREMONY EXPENSE TRACKER					
	BUDGET	COST	DEPOSIT	BALANCE	DUE DATE
OFFICIANT GRATUITY					
MARRIAGE LICENSE					
VENUE COST					
FLOWERS					
DECORATIONS					
OTHER					

NOTES & Reminders

NOTES & REMINDERS

RECEPTION EXPENSE TRACKER					
	BUDGET	COST	DEPOSIT	BALANCE	DUE DATE
VENUE FEE					
CATERING/FOOD					
BAR/BEVERAGES					
CAKE/CUTTING FEE					
DECORATIONS					
RENTALS/EXTRAS					
BARTENDER/STAFF					

NOTES & More

SPECIAL REMINDERS

Planning Snapshot

PAPER PRODUCTS EXPENSE TRACKER

	BUDGET	COST	DEPOSIT	BALANCE	DUE DATE
INVITATIONS/CARDS					
POSTAGE COSTS					
THANK YOU CARDS					
PLACE CARDS					
GUESTBOOK					
OTHER					

NOTES & Reminders

NOTES & REMINDERS

ENTERTAINMENT EXPENSE TRACKER

	BUDGET	COST	DEPOSIT	BALANCE	DUE DATE
BAND/DJ					
SOUND SYSTEM RENTAL					
VENUE/DANCE RENTAL					
GRATUITIES					
OTHER:					
OTHER:					
OTHER:					

NOTES & More

SPECIAL REMINDERS

Planning Snapshot

WEDDING PARTY ATTIRE EXPENSE TRACKER

	BUDGET	COST	DEPOSIT	BALANCE	DUE DATE
WEDDING DRESS					
TUX RENTALS					
BRIDESMAID DRESSES					
SHOES/HEELS					
VEIL/GARTER/OTHER					
ALTERATION COSTS					

NOTES & Reminders

NOTES & REMINDERS

TRANSPORTATION EXPENSE TRACKER

	BUDGET	COST	DEPOSIT	BALANCE	DUE DATE
LIMO RENTAL					
VALET PARKING					
VENUE TRANSPORTATION					
AIRPORT TRANSPORTATION					
OTHER:					
OTHER:					
OTHER:					

NOTES & More

SPECIAL REMINDERS

Planning Snapshot

FLORIST EXPENSE TRACKER

	BUDGET	COST	DEPOSIT	BALANCE	DUE DATE
BOUQUETS					
VENUE DECORATIONS					
BOUTONNIERES					
VASES/EXTRAS					
TABLE DECORATIONS					
OTHER:					

NOTES & Reminders

NOTES & REMINDERS

OTHER EXPENSE TRACKER

	BUDGET	COST	DEPOSIT	BALANCE	DUE DATE
PHOTOGRAPHER					
VIDEOGRAPHER					
CATERER					
HAIR/MAKEUP/SALON					
WEDDING RINGS					
WEDDING PARTY GIFTS					
OTHER:					

NOTES & More

SPECIAL REMINDERS

Bride's Planner

HAIR APPOINTMENT

SALON NAME	DATE	TIME	BOOKED FOR:		ADDRESS:
				☐	
				☐	
				☐	

NOTES	

MAKE UP APPOINTMENT

SALON NAME	DATE	TIME	BOOKED FOR:		ADDRESS:
				☐	
				☐	
				☐	

NOTES	

MANICURE/PEDICURE APPOINTMENT

SALON NAME	DATE	TIME	BOOKED FOR:		ADDRESS:
				☐	
				☐	
				☐	

NOTES	

Groom's Planner

HAIR APPOINTMENT

SALON NAME	DATE	TIME	BOOKED FOR:	ADDRESS:
			☐	
			☐	
			☐	

NOTES	

TUX FITTING APPOINTMENT

BUSINESS NAME	DATE	TIME	BOOKED FOR:	ADDRESS:
			☐	
			☐	

NOTES	

OTHER:

BUSINESS NAME	DATE	TIME	BOOKED FOR:	ADDRESS:
			☐	
			☐	
			☐	

NOTES	

Important Dates

DATE:	DATE:	DATE:	REMINDERS

DATE:	DATE:	DATE:

DATE:	DATE:	DATE:

NOTES

DATE:	DATE:	DATE:

DATE:	DATE:	DATE:

Weekly Wedding Planning

WEEK OF: _____

MONDAY

TUESDAY

WEDNESDAY

THURSDAY

FRIDAY

SATURDAY

WEDDING TO DO LIST

- ☐ _____
- ☐ _____
- ☐ _____
- ☐ _____
- ☐ _____
- ☐ _____
- ☐ _____
- ☐ _____
- ☐ _____
- ☐ _____
- ☐ _____
- ☐ _____
- ☐ _____
- ☐ _____
- ☐ _____
- ☐ _____

APPOINTMENTS & MEETINGS			
DATE	TIME	VENDOR	PURPOSE

Weekly Wedding Planning

WEEK OF: _____

MONDAY

TUESDAY

WEDNESDAY

THURSDAY

FRIDAY

SATURDAY

WEDDING TO DO LIST

- ☐ _____
- ☐ _____
- ☐ _____
- ☐ _____
- ☐ _____
- ☐ _____
- ☐ _____
- ☐ _____
- ☐ _____
- ☐ _____
- ☐ _____
- ☐ _____
- ☐ _____
- ☐ _____
- ☐ _____
- ☐ _____

APPOINTMENTS & MEETINGS

DATE	TIME	VENDOR	PURPOSE

Weekly Wedding Planning

WEEK OF: _____

MONDAY

TUESDAY

WEDNESDAY

THURSDAY

FRIDAY

SATURDAY

WEDDING TO DO LIST

- ☐ _____
- ☐ _____
- ☐ _____
- ☐ _____
- ☐ _____
- ☐ _____
- ☐ _____
- ☐ _____
- ☐ _____
- ☐ _____
- ☐ _____
- ☐ _____
- ☐ _____
- ☐ _____
- ☐ _____
- ☐ _____

APPOINTMENTS & MEETINGS			
DATE	TIME	VENDOR	PURPOSE

Weekly Wedding Planning

WEEK OF: _____

MONDAY

TUESDAY

WEDNESDAY

THURSDAY

FRIDAY

SATURDAY

WEDDING TO DO LIST

☐ _____
☐ _____
☐ _____
☐ _____
☐ _____
☐ _____
☐ _____
☐ _____
☐ _____
☐ _____
☐ _____
☐ _____
☐ _____
☐ _____
☐ _____

APPOINTMENTS & MEETINGS			
DATE	TIME	VENDOR	PURPOSE

Weekly Wedding Planning

WEEK OF: _____

MONDAY

TUESDAY

WEDNESDAY

THURSDAY

FRIDAY

SATURDAY

WEDDING TO DO LIST

- ☐ _____
- ☐ _____
- ☐ _____
- ☐ _____
- ☐ _____
- ☐ _____
- ☐ _____
- ☐ _____
- ☐ _____
- ☐ _____
- ☐ _____
- ☐ _____
- ☐ _____
- ☐ _____
- ☐ _____
- ☐ _____

APPOINTMENTS & MEETINGS

DATE	TIME	VENDOR	PURPOSE

Weekly Wedding Planning

WEEK OF: _____

MONDAY

TUESDAY

WEDNESDAY

THURSDAY

FRIDAY

SATURDAY

WEDDING TO DO LIST

- ☐ _____
- ☐ _____
- ☐ _____
- ☐ _____
- ☐ _____
- ☐ _____
- ☐ _____
- ☐ _____
- ☐ _____
- ☐ _____
- ☐ _____
- ☐ _____
- ☐ _____
- ☐ _____
- ☐ _____

APPOINTMENTS & MEETINGS

DATE	TIME	VENDOR	PURPOSE

Weekly Wedding Planning

WEEK OF: _____

MONDAY

TUESDAY

WEDNESDAY

THURSDAY

FRIDAY

SATURDAY

WEDDING TO DO LIST

- [ ] _____
- [ ] _____
- [ ] _____
- [ ] _____
- [ ] _____
- [ ] _____
- [ ] _____
- [ ] _____
- [ ] _____
- [ ] _____
- [ ] _____
- [ ] _____
- [ ] _____
- [ ] _____
- [ ] _____

APPOINTMENTS & MEETINGS

DATE	TIME	VENDOR	PURPOSE

Weekly Wedding Planning

WEEK OF: _____

MONDAY

TUESDAY

WEDNESDAY

THURSDAY

FRIDAY

SATURDAY

WEDDING TO DO LIST

- [ ]
- [ ]
- [ ]
- [ ]
- [ ]
- [ ]
- [ ]
- [ ]
- [ ]
- [ ]
- [ ]
- [ ]
- [ ]
- [ ]
- [ ]
- [ ]

APPOINTMENTS & MEETINGS

DATE	TIME	VENDOR	PURPOSE

Weekly Wedding Planning

WEEK OF: _____

MONDAY

TUESDAY

WEDNESDAY

THURSDAY

FRIDAY

SATURDAY

WEDDING TO DO LIST

- ☐ _____
- ☐ _____
- ☐ _____
- ☐ _____
- ☐ _____
- ☐ _____
- ☐ _____
- ☐ _____
- ☐ _____
- ☐ _____
- ☐ _____
- ☐ _____
- ☐ _____
- ☐ _____
- ☐ _____

APPOINTMENTS & MEETINGS

DATE	TIME	VENDOR	PURPOSE

Weekly Wedding Planning

WEEK OF: ....

MONDAY

TUESDAY

WEDNESDAY

THURSDAY

FRIDAY

SATURDAY

WEDDING TO DO LIST

- [ ] _____
- [ ] _____
- [ ] _____
- [ ] _____
- [ ] _____
- [ ] _____
- [ ] _____
- [ ] _____
- [ ] _____
- [ ] _____
- [ ] _____
- [ ] _____
- [ ] _____
- [ ] _____
- [ ] _____
- [ ] _____

APPOINTMENTS & MEETINGS

DATE	TIME	VENDOR	PURPOSE

Weekly Wedding Planning

WEEK OF: _____

MONDAY

TUESDAY

WEDNESDAY

THURSDAY

FRIDAY

SATURDAY

WEDDING TO DO LIST

- ☐ _____
- ☐ _____
- ☐ _____
- ☐ _____
- ☐ _____
- ☐ _____
- ☐ _____
- ☐ _____
- ☐ _____
- ☐ _____
- ☐ _____
- ☐ _____
- ☐ _____
- ☐ _____
- ☐ _____
- ☐ _____

APPOINTMENTS & MEETINGS

DATE	TIME	VENDOR	PURPOSE

Weekly Wedding Planning

WEEK OF: _____

MONDAY

WEDDING TO DO LIST

- [ ] _____
- [ ] _____
- [ ] _____
- [ ] _____
- [ ] _____
- [ ] _____
- [ ] _____
- [ ] _____
- [ ] _____
- [ ] _____
- [ ] _____
- [ ] _____
- [ ] _____
- [ ] _____
- [ ] _____

TUESDAY

WEDNESDAY

THURSDAY

APPOINTMENTS & MEETINGS			
DATE	TIME	VENDOR	PURPOSE

FRIDAY

SATURDAY

Weekly Wedding Planning

WEEK OF: _____

MONDAY

TUESDAY

WEDNESDAY

THURSDAY

FRIDAY

SATURDAY

WEDDING TO DO LIST

- ☐ _____
- ☐ _____
- ☐ _____
- ☐ _____
- ☐ _____
- ☐ _____
- ☐ _____
- ☐ _____
- ☐ _____
- ☐ _____
- ☐ _____
- ☐ _____
- ☐ _____
- ☐ _____
- ☐ _____
- ☐ _____

APPOINTMENTS & MEETINGS			
DATE	TIME	VENDOR	PURPOSE

Weekly Wedding Planning

WEEK OF: _____

MONDAY

TUESDAY

WEDNESDAY

THURSDAY

FRIDAY

SATURDAY

WEDDING TO DO LIST

- [ ] _____
- [ ] _____
- [ ] _____
- [ ] _____
- [ ] _____
- [ ] _____
- [ ] _____
- [ ] _____
- [ ] _____
- [ ] _____
- [ ] _____
- [ ] _____
- [ ] _____
- [ ] _____
- [ ] _____
- [ ] _____

APPOINTMENTS & MEETINGS

DATE	TIME	VENDOR	PURPOSE

Weekly Wedding Planning

WEEK OF: _____

MONDAY

WEDDING TO DO LIST

- [ ] _____
- [ ] _____
- [ ] _____
- [ ] _____
- [ ] _____
- [ ] _____
- [ ] _____
- [ ] _____
- [ ] _____
- [ ] _____
- [ ] _____
- [ ] _____
- [ ] _____
- [ ] _____
- [ ] _____
- [ ] _____

TUESDAY

WEDNESDAY

THURSDAY

APPOINTMENTS & MEETINGS

DATE	TIME	VENDOR	PURPOSE

FRIDAY

SATURDAY

Weekly Wedding Planning

WEEK OF: _____

MONDAY

TUESDAY

WEDNESDAY

THURSDAY

FRIDAY

SATURDAY

WEDDING TO DO LIST

- [ ] _____
- [ ] _____
- [ ] _____
- [ ] _____
- [ ] _____
- [ ] _____
- [ ] _____
- [ ] _____
- [ ] _____
- [ ] _____
- [ ] _____
- [ ] _____
- [ ] _____
- [ ] _____
- [ ] _____
- [ ] _____

APPOINTMENTS & MEETINGS

DATE	TIME	VENDOR	PURPOSE

Weekly Wedding Planning

WEEK OF: _____

MONDAY

TUESDAY

WEDNESDAY

THURSDAY

FRIDAY

SATURDAY

WEDDING TO DO LIST

- ☐ _____
- ☐ _____
- ☐ _____
- ☐ _____
- ☐ _____
- ☐ _____
- ☐ _____
- ☐ _____
- ☐ _____
- ☐ _____
- ☐ _____
- ☐ _____
- ☐ _____
- ☐ _____
- ☐ _____

APPOINTMENTS & MEETINGS

DATE	TIME	VENDOR	PURPOSE

Weekly Wedding Planning

WEEK OF: _____

MONDAY

TUESDAY

WEDNESDAY

THURSDAY

FRIDAY

SATURDAY

WEDDING TO DO LIST

- [ ] _____
- [ ] _____
- [ ] _____
- [ ] _____
- [ ] _____
- [ ] _____
- [ ] _____
- [ ] _____
- [ ] _____
- [ ] _____
- [ ] _____
- [ ] _____
- [ ] _____
- [ ] _____
- [ ] _____

APPOINTMENTS & MEETINGS

DATE	TIME	VENDOR	PURPOSE

Weekly Wedding Planning

WEEK OF: _____

MONDAY

TUESDAY

WEDNESDAY

THURSDAY

FRIDAY

SATURDAY

WEDDING TO DO LIST

☐ _____
☐ _____
☐ _____
☐ _____
☐ _____
☐ _____
☐ _____
☐ _____
☐ _____
☐ _____
☐ _____
☐ _____
☐ _____
☐ _____
☐ _____
☐ _____

APPOINTMENTS & MEETINGS			
DATE	TIME	VENDOR	PURPOSE

Weekly Wedding Planning

WEEK OF: ....

MONDAY

TUESDAY

WEDNESDAY

THURSDAY

FRIDAY

SATURDAY

WEDDING TO DO LIST

- [ ] _____
- [ ] _____
- [ ] _____
- [ ] _____
- [ ] _____
- [ ] _____
- [ ] _____
- [ ] _____
- [ ] _____
- [ ] _____
- [ ] _____
- [ ] _____
- [ ] _____
- [ ] _____
- [ ] _____

APPOINTMENTS & MEETINGS			
DATE	TIME	VENDOR	PURPOSE

Wedding Planner

- PLANNING GUIDELINE -

12 Months BEFORE WEDDING

- ☐ SET THE DATE
- ☐ SET YOUR BUDGET
- ☐ CONSIDER WEDDING THEMES
- ☐ PLAN ENGAGEMENT PARTY
- ☐ RESEARCH POSSIBLE VENUES
- ☐ START RESEARCHING GOWNS
- ☐ RESEARCH PHOTOGRAPHERS
- ☐ RESEARCH VIDEOGRAPHERS
- ☐ RESEARCH DJS/ENTERTAINMENT

- ☐ CONSIDER FLORISTS
- ☐ RESEARCH CATERERS
- ☐ DECIDE ON OFFICIANT
- ☐ CREATE INITIAL GUEST LIST
- ☐ CHOOSE WEDDING PARTY
- ☐ CONSIDER ACCESSORIES
- ☐ REGISTER WITH GIFT REGISTRY
- ☐ DISCUSS HONEYMOON IDEAS
- ☐ RESEARCH WEDDING RINGS

- ☐ CONSIDER MUSIC CHOICES
- ☐ DECIDE ON OFFICIANT
- ☐ CONSIDER TRANSPORTATION
- ☐ CREATE INITIAL GUEST LIST
- ☐ CHOOSE WEDDING PARTY
- ☐ BRIDEMAIDS GOWNS
- ☐ BOOK TENTATIVE HOTELS
- ☐ CONSIDER BEAUTY SALONS
- ☐ CONSIDER SHOES & OTHER

Things To Do	Status

TOP PRIORITIES

NOTES & IDEAS

APPOINTMENTS & REMINDERS

Wedding Planner

- PLANNING GUIDELINE -

- FINALIZE GUEST LIST
- ORDER INVITATIONS
- PLAN YOUR RECEPTION
- BOOK PHOTOGRAPHER
- BOOK VIDEOGRAPHER
- CHOOSE WEDDING GOWN

- ORDER BRIDESMAIDS DRESSES
- RESERVE TUXEDOS
- ARRANGE TRANSPORTATION
- BOOK WEDDING VENUE
- BOOK RECEPTION VENUE
- PLAN HONEYMOON

- BOOK FLORIST
- BOOK DJ/ENTERTAINMENT
- BOOK CATERER
- CHOOSE WEDDING CAKE
- BOOK OFFICIANT
- BOOK ROOMS FOR GUESTS

Things To Do	Status

TOP PRIORITIES

NOTES & IDEAS

APPOINTMENTS & REMINDERS

Wedding Planner

6 Months BEFORE WEDDING

- PLANNING GUIDELINE -

- ☐ ORDER THANK YOU NOTES
- ☐ REVIEW RECEPTION DETAILS
- ☐ MAKE APPT FOR FITTING
- ☐ CONFIRM BRIDAL DRESSES
- ☐ OBTAIN MARRIAGE LICENSE
- ☐ BOOK HAIR STYLIST

- ☐ BOOK NAIL SALON
- ☐ CONFIRM MUSIC SELECTION
- ☐ WRITE VOWS
- ☐ PLAN BRIDAL SHOWER
- ☐ PLAN REHEARSAL
- ☐ BOOK REHEARSAL DINNER

- ☐ SHOP FOR WEDDING RINGS
- ☐ PLAN DECORATIONS
- ☐ CHOOSE BOUQUET TYPE
- ☐ FINALIZE GUEST LIST
- ☐ UPDATE PASSPORTS
- ☐ CONFIRM HOTEL ROOMS

Things To Do	Status

TOP PRIORITIES

NOTES & IDEAS

APPOINTMENTS & REMINDERS

Wedding Planner

- PLANNING GUIDELINE -

- ☐ MAIL OUT INVITATIONS
- ☐ MEET WITH OFFICIANT
- ☐ BUY WEDDING FAVORS
- ☐ BUY WEDDING PARTY GIFTS
- ☐ PURCHASE SHOES
- ☐ FINALIZE THANK YOU CARDS

- ☐ FINALIZE HONEYMOON PLANS
- ☐ ATTEND FIRST DRESS FITTING
- ☐ FINALIZE VOWS
- ☐ FINALIZE RECEPTION MENU
- ☐ KEEP TRACK OF RSVPS
- ☐ BOOK PHOTO SESSION

- ☐ CONFIRM CATERER
- ☐ FINALIZE RING FITTING
- ☐ CONFIRM FLOWERS
- ☐ CONFIRM BAND
- ☐ SHOP FOR HONEYMOON
- ☐ BUY GARTER BELT

Things To Do	Status

TOP PRIORITIES

NOTES & IDEAS

APPOINTMENTS & REMINDERS

Wedding Planner

- PLANNING GUIDELINE -

- ☐ CHOOSE YOUR MC
- ☐ REQUEST SPECIAL TOASTS
- ☐ ARRANGE TRANSPORTATION
- ☐ CHOOSE YOUR HAIR STYLE
- ☐ CHOOSE YOUR NAIL COLOR
- ☐ ATTEND BRIDAL SHOWER

- ☐ CONFIRM CAKE CHOICES
- ☐ CONFIRM MENU (FINAL)
- ☐ CONFIRM SEATING
- ☐ CONFIRM VIDEOGRAPHER
- ☐ ARRANGE LEGAL DOCS
- ☐ FINALIZE WEDDING DUTIES

- ☐ CONFIRM BRIDESMAID DRESSES
- ☐ MEET WITH DJ/MC
- ☐ FINAL DRESS FITTING
- ☐ WRAP WEDDING PARTY GIFTS
- ☐ CONFIRM FINAL GUEST COUNT
- ☐ CREATE WEDDING SCHEDULE

Things To Do	Status

TOP PRIORITIES

NOTES & IDEAS

APPOINTMENTS & REMINDERS

Wedding Planner

- PLANNING GUIDELINE -

- ☐ PAYMENT TO VENDORS
- ☐ PACK FOR HONEYMOON
- ☐ CONFIRM HOTEL RESERVATION
- ☐ GIVE SCHEDULE TO PARTY
- ☐ DELIVER LICENSE TO OFFICIANT
- ☐ CONFIRM WITH VENDORS

- ☐ PICK UP WEDDING DRESS
- ☐ PICK UP TUXEDOS
- ☐ GIVE MUSIC LIST TO DJ/BAND
- ☐ CONFIRM SHOES/HEELS FIT
- ☐ CONFIRM TRANSPORTATION
- ☐ MONEY FOR GRATUITIES

- ☐ COMPLETE MAKE UP TRIAL
- ☐ CONFIRM RINGS FIT
- ☐ CONFIRM TRAVEL PLANS
- ☐ CONFIRM HOTELS FOR GUESTS
- ☐ OTHER: _____
- ☐ OTHER: _____

Things To Do	Status

TOP PRIORITIES

♥

NOTES & IDEAS

♥

APPOINTMENTS & REMINDERS

Wedding Planner

- PLANNING GUIDELINE -

1 Day BEFORE WEDDING

- ☐ ATTEND REHEARSAL DINNER
- ☐ FINISH HONEYMOON PACKING
- ☐ GREET OUT OF TOWN GUESTS

- ☐ GET MANICURE/PEDICURE
- ☐ CHECK ON WEDDING VENUE
- ☐ CHECK WEATHER TO PREPARE

- ☐ GIVE GIFTS TO WEDDING PARTY
- ☐ CONFIRM RINGS FIT
- ☐ GET A GOOD NIGHT'S SLEEP

Things To Do	Status

TOP PRIORITIES

♥

NOTES & IDEAS

♥

APPOINTMENTS & REMINDERS

Your Special Day!

Day of WEDDING

- ☐ GET YOUR HAIR DONE
- ☐ GET YOUR MAKE UP DONE

- ☐ HAVE A LIGHT BREAKFAST
- ☐ MEET WITH BRIDAL PARTY

- ☐ GIVE RINGS TO BEST MAN
- ☐ ENJOY YOUR SPECIAL DAY!

MR ♥ MRS

Wedding Attire Planner

WEDDING ATTIRE EXPENSE TRACKER

ITEM/PURCHASE	STATUS ✓	DATE PAID	TOTAL COST

NOTES & REMINDERS	TOTAL COST:

Notes:

WEDDING ATTIRE DETAILS

Venue Planner

VENUE EXPENSE TRACKER

ITEM/PURCHASE	STATUS ✓	DATE PAID	TOTAL COST

NOTES & REMINDERS	
	TOTAL COST:

Notes:

VENUE PLANNING DETAILS

Catering Planner

CATERING EXPENSE TRACKER

ITEM/PURCHASE	STATUS ✓	DATE PAID	TOTAL COST

NOTES & REMINDERS	
	TOTAL COST:

Notes:

....

....

....

....

....

....

....

....

CATERING PLANNER DETAILS

Entertainment Planner

ENTERTAINMENT EXPENSE TRACKER			
ITEM/PURCHASE	STATUS ✓	DATE PAID	TOTAL COST

NOTES & REMINDERS

TOTAL COST:

Notes:

Love

ENTERTAINMENT DETAILS

Videographer Planner

VIDEOGRAPHER EXPENSE TRACKER

ITEM/PURCHASE	STATUS ✓	DATE PAID	TOTAL COST
☐			
☐			
☐			
☐			
☐			

NOTES & REMINDERS

TOTAL COST:

Notes:

....
....
....
....
....
....
....
....

VIDEOGRAPHER DETAILS

Photographer Planner

PHOTOGRAPHER EXPENSE TRACKER

ITEM/PURCHASE	STATUS ✓	DATE PAID	TOTAL COST

NOTES & REMINDERS	
	TOTAL COST:

Notes:

PHOTOGRAPHER DETAILS

Florist Planner

FLORIST EXPENSE TRACKER

ITEM/PURCHASE	STATUS ✓	DATE PAID	TOTAL COST

NOTES & REMINDERS

TOTAL COST:

Notes:

_____

_____

_____

_____

_____

_____

_____

_____

FLORIST PLANNING DETAILS

Extra Wedding Costs

MISC WEDDING EXPENSE TRACKER			
ITEM/PURCHASE	STATUS ✓	DATE PAID	TOTAL COST

NOTES & REMINDERS

TOTAL COST:

Notes:

....
....
....
....
....
....
....
....
....

MISC WEDDING DETAILS

Bachelorette Party Planner

EVENT DETAILS

DATE

TIME

VENUE

THEME

HOST

OTHER

TIME	SCHEDULE OF EVENTS

NOTES & REMINDERS

love

GUEST LIST

FIRST NAME	LAST NAME	RVSP

SUPPLIES & SHOPPING LIST

- [ ]
- [ ]
- [ ]
- [ ]
- [ ]
- [ ]
- [ ]
- [ ]
- [ ]
- [ ]
- [ ]
- [ ]
- [ ]
- [ ]
- [ ]
- [ ]

Bachelor Party Planner

EVENT DETAILS

DATE

TIME

VENUE

THEME

HOST

OTHER

GUEST LIST

FIRST NAME	LAST NAME	RVSP

TIME	SCHEDULE OF EVENTS

SUPPLIES & SHOPPING LIST

- [ ]
- [ ]
- [ ]
- [ ]
- [ ]
- [ ]
- [ ]
- [ ]
- [ ]
- [ ]
- [ ]
- [ ]
- [ ]
- [ ]
- [ ]
- [ ]
- [ ]

NOTES & REMINDERS

love

Reception Planner

MEAL PLANNER IDEAS

HORS D'OEUVRES

1st COURSE:

3rd COURSE:

2nd COURSE:

4th COURSE:

MEAL PLANNING NOTES

Wedding Planning Notes

IDEAS & REMINDERS

Wedding to do List

PLANNING FOR THE BIG DAY

Wedding Guest List

NAME	ADDRESS	PHONE #	# IN PARTY	RSVP: ✓

Wedding Guest List

NAME	ADDRESS	PHONE #	# IN PARTY	RSVP: ✓

Wedding Guest List

NAME	ADDRESS	PHONE #	# IN PARTY	RSVP: ✓

Wedding Guest List

NAME	ADDRESS	PHONE #	# IN PARTY	RSVP: ✓

Wedding Guest List

NAME	ADDRESS	PHONE #	# IN PARTY	RSVP: ✓

Wedding Guest List

NAME	ADDRESS	PHONE #	# IN PARTY	RSVP: ✓

Wedding Guest List

NAME	ADDRESS	PHONE #	# IN PARTY	RSVP: ✓

Wedding Guest List

NAME	ADDRESS	PHONE #	# IN PARTY	RSVP: ✓

Wedding Guest List

NAME	ADDRESS	PHONE #	# IN PARTY	RSVP: ✓

Wedding Guest List

NAME	ADDRESS	PHONE #	# IN PARTY	RSVP: ✓

Wedding Seating Chart

Table #

TABLE #:
1 :
2 :
3 :
4 :
5 :
6 :
7 :
8 :

Table #

TABLE #:
1 :
2 :
3 :
4 :
5 :
6 :
7 :
8 :

Wedding Seating Chart

Table #

Table #

TABLE #:	
1 :	
2 :	
3 :	
4 :	
5 :	
6 :	
7 :	
8 :	

love

TABLE #:	
1 :	
2 :	
3 :	
4 :	
5 :	
6 :	
7 :	
8 :	

Wedding Seating Chart

Table #

Table #

TABLE #:

1:

2:

3:

4:

5:

6:

7:

8:

TABLE #:

1:

2:

3:

4:

5:

6:

7:

8:

Wedding Seating Chart

Table #

Table #

TABLE #:

1 :

2 :

3 :

4 :

5 :

6 :

7 :

8 :

TABLE #:

1 :

2 :

3 :

4 :

5 :

6 :

7 :

8 :

Wedding Seating Chart

Table #

Table #

TABLE #:
1:
2:
3:
4:
5:
6:
7:
8:

TABLE #:
1:
2:
3:
4:
5:
6:
7:
8:

Wedding Seating Chart

Table #

Table #

TABLE #:
1:
2:
3:
4:
5:
6:
7:
8:

TABLE #:
1:
2:
3:
4:
5:
6:
7:
8:

Wedding Seating Chart

Table #

Table #

TABLE #:
1 :
2 :
3 :
4 :
5 :
6 :
7 :
8 :

TABLE #:
1 :
2 :
3 :
4 :
5 :
6 :
7 :
8 :

Wedding Seating Chart

Table #

Table #

TABLE #:

1 :

2 :

3 :

4 :

5 :

6 :

7 :

8 :

TABLE #:

1 :

2 :

3 :

4 :

5 :

6 :

7 :

8 :

Wedding Seating Chart

Table #

Table #

TABLE #:
1 :
2 :
3 :
4 :
5 :
6 :
7 :
8 :

TABLE #:
1 :
2 :
3 :
4 :
5 :
6 :
7 :
8 :

Wedding Seating Chart

Table #

Table #

TABLE #:

1 :

2 :

3 :

4 :

5 :

6 :

7 :

8 :

TABLE #:

1 :

2 :

3 :

4 :

5 :

6 :

7 :

8 :

Wedding Seating Chart

Table #

Table #

TABLE #:
1 :
2 :
3 :
4 :
5 :
6 :
7 :
8 :

TABLE #:
1 :
2 :
3 :
4 :
5 :
6 :
7 :
8 :

Wedding Seating Chart

Table #

Table #

TABLE #:
1 :
2 :
3 :
4 :
5 :
6 :
7 :
8 :

TABLE #:
1 :
2 :
3 :
4 :
5 :
6 :
7 :
8 :

Wedding Seating Chart

Table #

Table #

TABLE #:

1:

2:

3:

4:

5:

6:

7:

8:

TABLE #:

1:

2:

3:

4:

5:

6:

7:

8:

Wedding Seating Chart

Table #

Table #

TABLE #:
1 :
2 :
3 :
4 :
5 :
6 :
7 :
8 :

TABLE #:
1 :
2 :
3 :
4 :
5 :
6 :
7 :
8 :

Wedding Seating Chart

Table #

Table #

TABLE #:

1:

2:

3:

4:

5:

6:

7:

8:

TABLE #:

1:

2:

3:

4:

5:

6:

7:

8:

Wedding Seating Chart

Table #

Table #

TABLE #:

1:

2:

3:

4:

5:

6:

7:

8:

TABLE #:

1:

2:

3:

4:

5:

6:

7:

8:

Wedding Seating Chart

Table #

Table #

TABLE #:

1 :

2 :

3 :

4 :

5 :

6 :

7 :

8 :

TABLE #:

1 :

2 :

3 :

4 :

5 :

6 :

7 :

8 :

Wedding Seating Chart

Table #

Table #

TABLE #:
1 :
2 :
3 :
4 :
5 :
6 :
7 :
8 :

TABLE #:
1 :
2 :
3 :
4 :
5 :
6 :
7 :
8 :

Wedding Seating Chart

Table #

TABLE #:	
1:	
2:	
3:	
4:	
5:	
6:	
7:	
8:	

Table #

TABLE #:	
1:	
2:	
3:	
4:	
5:	
6:	
7:	
8:	

Wedding Seating Chart

Table #

Table #

TABLE #:
1 :
2 :
3 :
4 :
5 :
6 :
7 :
8 :

Wedding Seating Chart

Table #

Table #

TABLE #:
1 :
2 :
3 :
4 :
5 :
6 :
7 :
8 :

TABLE #:
1 :
2 :
3 :
4 :
5 :
6 :
7 :
8 :

Wedding Seating Chart

Table #

Table #

TABLE #:

1 :

2 :

3 :

4 :

5 :

6 :

7 :

8 :

TABLE #:

1 :

2 :

3 :

4 :

5 :

6 :

7 :

8 :

Wedding Seating Chart

Table #

Table #

TABLE #:

1 :

2 :

3 :

4 :

5 :

6 :

7 :

8 :

TABLE #:

1 :

2 :

3 :

4 :

5 :

6 :

7 :

8 :

Wedding Seating Chart

Table #

Table #

TABLE #:

1 :

2 :

3 :

4 :

5 :

6 :

7 :

8 :

TABLE #:

1 :

2 :

3 :

4 :

5 :

6 :

7 :

8 :

Wedding Seating Chart

Table #

Table #

TABLE #:

1:

2:

3:

4:

5:

6:

7:

8:

TABLE #:

1:

2:

3:

4:

5:

6:

7:

8:

Wedding Seating Chart

Table #

Table #

TABLE #:
1 :
2 :
3 :
4 :
5 :
6 :
7 :
8 :

TABLE #:
1 :
2 :
3 :
4 :
5 :
6 :
7 :
8 :

Wedding Seating Chart

Table #

TABLE #:

1:	2:	3:	4:	5:	6:	7:	8:
9:	10:	11:	12:	13:	14:	15:	16:

Table #

TABLE #:

1:	2:	3:	4:	5:	6:	7:	8:
9:	10:	11:	12:	13:	14:	15:	16:

Wedding Seating Chart

Table #

TABLE #:

1:	2:	3:	4:	5:	6:	7:	8:
9:	10:	11:	12:	13:	14:	15:	16:

Table #

TABLE #:

1:	2:	3:	4:	5:	6:	7:	8:
9:	10:	11:	12:	13:	14:	15:	16:

Wedding Seating Chart

Table

TABLE #:

1:	2:	3:	4:	5:	6:	7:	8:
9:	10:	11:	12:	13:	14:	15:	16:

Table

TABLE #:

1:	2:	3:	4:	5:	6:	7:	8:
9:	10:	11:	12:	13:	14:	15:	16:

Wedding Seating Chart

Table

TABLE #:

1:	2:	3:	4:	5:	6:	7:	8:
9:	10:	11:	12:	13:	14:	15:	16:

Table

TABLE #:

1:	2:	3:	4:	5:	6:	7:	8:
9:	10:	11:	12:	13:	14:	15:	16:

Wedding Seating Chart

Table

TABLE #:

1:	2:	3:	4:	5:	6:	7:	8:
9:	10:	11:	12:	13:	14:	15:	16:

Table

TABLE #:

1:	2:	3:	4:	5:	6:	7:	8:
9:	10:	11:	12:	13:	14:	15:	16:

Wedding Seating Chart

Table

TABLE #:

1:	2:	3:	4:	5:	6:	7:	8:
9:	10:	11:	12:	13:	14:	15:	16:

Table

TABLE #:

1:	2:	3:	4:	5:	6:	7:	8:
9:	10:	11:	12:	13:	14:	15:	16:

Wedding Seating Chart

Table

TABLE #:

1:	2:	3:	4:	5:	6:	7:	8:
9:	10:	11:	12:	13:	14:	15:	16:

Table

TABLE #:

1:	2:	3:	4:	5:	6:	7:	8:
9:	10:	11:	12:	13:	14:	15:	16:

Wedding Seating Chart

Table #

TABLE #:

1:	2:	3:	4:	5:	6:	7:	8:
9:	10:	11:	12:	13:	14:	15:	16:

Table #

TABLE #:

1:	2:	3:	4:	5:	6:	7:	8:
9:	10:	11:	12:	13:	14:	15:	16:

Wedding Seating Chart

Table

TABLE #:

1:	2:	3:	4:	5:	6:	7:	8:
9:	10:	11:	12:	13:	14:	15:	16:

Table

TABLE #:

1:	2:	3:	4:	5:	6:	7:	8:
9:	10:	11:	12:	13:	14:	15:	16:

Wedding Seating Chart

Table #

TABLE #:

1:	2:	3:	4:	5:	6:	7:	8:
9:	10:	11:	12:	13:	14:	15:	16:

Table #

TABLE #:

1:	2:	3:	4:	5:	6:	7:	8:
9:	10:	11:	12:	13:	14:	15:	16:

Wedding Seating Chart

Table #

TABLE #:

1:	2:	3:	4:	5:	6:	7:	8:
9:	10:	11:	12:	13:	14:	15:	16:

Table #

TABLE #:

1:	2:	3:	4:	5:	6:	7:	8:
9:	10:	11:	12:	13:	14:	15:	16:

Made in the USA
Columbia, SC
06 April 2020

90665839R00057